WALT DISNEY PRODUCTIONS
presents

GOOFY'S GAGS

Random House New York

Library of Congress Cataloging in Publication Data

Walt Disney Productions presents Goofy's gags.
(Disney's wonderful world of reading, #19)
Goofy stars in an easy-to-read collection of riddles.
1. Riddles. [1. Riddles] I. Disney (Walt) Productions. II. Title: Goofy's gags. PZ8.7.W3
398.6 74-2043 ISBN 0-394-82558-6 ISBN 0-394-92558-0 (lib. bdg.)

Manufactured in the United States of America

B   C   D   E   F   G   H   I   J   K
4

What does a cowboy say at the end of a long ride?

Whoa!

What does Santa say when he works
in his garden?

Hoe, Hoe, Hoe!

What do birds say on Halloween?

Trick or tweet.

Why do birds fly south
for the winter?

It's too far to walk.

What is brown, has a hump,
and lives at the North Pole?

Rudolph the Red-Nosed Camel.

Where is the best place
to crown a king?

On the head.

What do you get
when you cross...

1   a chicken   and   a bell?

2   a cow   and   a pogo stick?

3   a worm   and   a fur coat?

4   two pizzas   and   handlebars?

5   a cactus   and   a porcupine?

Turn the page to see the answers.

You get...

1 an alarm cluck.

2 a milkshake.

3 a caterpillar.

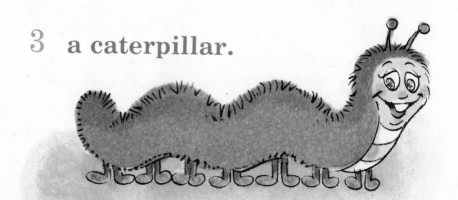

4 a pie-cycle.

5 sore hands.

What is the best month
for a parade?

March.

What goes
clomp, clomp,
clomp, clomp,
clomp, clomp,
clomp, squoosh?

An octopus with one shoe off.

How can four people go out under only one umbrella and not get wet?

It isn't raining.

What did the big firecracker say
to the little firecracker?

My pop is bigger than your pop.

What is a Boobee?

It's a little bug
that hides
in flowers

and scares bees.

When do elephants
have sixteen feet?

When there are four elephants.

Why did the elephant sit
on the marshmallow?

So he wouldn't fall in the cocoa.

What word has the most
letters in it?

Mailbox.

If you put a blue hat

in red punch,

what will it be?

Wet.

Why does a stork stand on one leg?

So it won't fall over.

Where were
Goofy's friends
when the lights
went out?

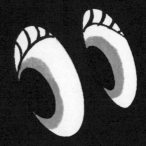

In the dark.